AF883712

LOVE BOT

Love in the Age of ChatGPT

Conversations for Connection, Compassion & Confidence

Sugar Gay Isber McMillan

The WOW Book Co.™
Austin, Texas

Love Bot: Love in the Age of ChatGPT

Conversations for Connection,

Compassion & Confidence

© 2025 Sugar Gay Isber McMillan.
All rights reserved.

No part of this publication may be reproduced, distributed, or transmitted in any form or by any means without the prior written permission of the publisher, except for brief quotations used in reviews or scholarly works.

All design, layout, text and editorial content are original works created by Sugar Gay Isber McMillan. No artificial intelligence or automated content-generation tools were used in the creation of the text or images within this book.

Printed in the United States of America on Amazon KDP on demand.

Large font edition.

U.S.-made materials and production.

ISBN: 978-1-967973-64-4

Published by **The WOW Book Co.™**, Austin, Texas

Series Note:
Love Bot is part of the *Talk to Your Tools™* series - practical, human-centered books that show how artificial intelligence can help people grow, create, and connect in the real world. Titles include *The Prompt Whisperer, Prompt Magic, Manifesting Bot, Skinny Bot, Rich Bot, Poor Bot, Santa Bot, Boomer Bot,* and *Atomic Bot.*

For more books by Sugar Gay Isber McMillan, visit
SugarGayIsberMcMillanBooks.com

Introduction | Let's Talk About Love

A modern guide to finding real connection in a digital world.

Love, wealth, and health. Those are the big three- the things most people wish for. Sure, a house and a car are nice, but let's be honest: it's love that keeps the lights on inside your heart.

Do you remember your first crush? I do. I was five years old on the playground, and a boy named Donald Patterson kissed my hand - or maybe he just wiped his nose on it. I didn't care. I was starstruck. He was adorable, and that tiny, confusing moment stuck with me my whole life. I learned early that attention feels like magic.

Fast forward a few decades, a few husbands, and more than a few heartbreaks later - and I can tell you this: love isn't luck. It's a strategy. It's the most human puzzle there is, and finding your match is a lot like finding the right job. It takes intention, a plan, and the right tools.

That's where this book-and your Love Bot - come in.

If you've ever found yourself lying awake at night whispering, *Please, just let me meet someone good,* I've been there. Twelve long years of being single in between marriages taught me a lot.

There were good moments and lonely ones. I hated seeing couples everywhere, at restaurants, at the grocery store, even walking dogs in pairs. It felt like the world was holding hands without me.

When I finally got serious about finding love again, I made a plan. I made a list - an honest one. Not just tall, dark, and handsome, but patient, kind, creative, and curious.

The funny thing? My husband turned out to be every single thing on that list, and one bonus I hadn't thought to ask for: he loves hockey. Who knew that mattered? Apparently, I did, deep down.

That's what this book will help you do: figure out what you *really* want, not what you think you should want.

You'll use your Love Bot (a.k.a. ChatGPT) to help you see yourself more clearly, refine your vision, and stay on track.

This is an inclusive book - it doesn't matter who you love. It matters that you love wisely, and that you love yourself along the way.

A few ground rules:

Don't make your first date a dinner. That's not a conversation, it's an audition.

Who wants to be interrupted by a waiter, be judged by what you ate, parsley in your teeth and the awkward moment when the bill arrives.

Coffee is perfect. Fifteen minutes. Meet, greet, move on.

If he shows up smelling bad or looking like he's been napping in his car - no, thank you. You deserve more.

Don't fall for potential. You're not a renovation project manager.

And for heaven's sake, don't give up after one bad date. There are billions of people on this planet. Someone's looking for you, too.

When it works, it won't be hard. It'll feel right. Effortless. Familiar. That's how you'll know.

So, let's talk about love and marriage, and all the beautiful chaos in between. Let's build a map for finding the right person, using modern tools and timeless wisdom.

You've already done the hardest part: you're still open to love. That means you're halfway there.

Before you can find love, you've got to find *you*. That's where this journey starts.

If you've been through heartbreak, boredom, or twelve years of Netflix alone (I've done it), your "love voice" may have gone quiet. Don't worry. We're about to bring it back—with a little help from your Love Bot.

Here's what we'll do next:

- Reboot your inner dialogue (you can't attract what you secretly argue with).
- Write a few truth lists - the *what I want* and *what I bring* kind.
- Learn how to use your chatbot as your sounding board.

- Practice real self-talk that builds confidence, not cringe.
- Start small, start honest, start now.

Your Love Bot isn't a dating coach.
It's your mirror, your cheerleader, and sometimes your best truth-teller.

So, grab your coffee, open your chat bot and get ready to type this simple prompt:

"Help me describe the kind of love that makes me feel safe, excited, and seen."

That's how it starts - one honest line, one real connection at a time.

Now, let's go find your voice again.

Chapter 1 | Finding Your Voice Again

Before love, there must be language.
Not the language of swipes or small talk, but the quiet, inner voice that tells you what you want, what you'll accept, and how you wish to be seen. For many of us, that voice has gone missing-drowned out by busy lives, heartbreak, or years of people-pleasing.

ChatGPT can't fall in love for you, but it can help you *hear yourself* again.

Think of it as your conversation mirror. When you start talking to your bot about how you feel, what went wrong, or what you hope for next, you start noticing the patterns. The tone you use. The stories you keep telling yourself. The silences that speak louder than words.

This is where love begins - by listening to yourself.

The 3 Stages of Re-Finding Your Voice

1. **Awareness.** Notice what you say when you describe yourself to others. Are you kind, or critical?
2. **Acceptance.** Write one sentence that begins, *"I am learning to..."* and finish it honestly.
3. **Affirmation.** Ask your bot to rephrase that sentence in a more loving way. Example:
    - You: "I am learning to trust that I can be loved again."
    - Your Bot: "You are worthy of a love that feels easy, honest, and true."

Read it aloud. Feel the difference? That's your new inner dialogue beginning to form.

Try This Prompt

Prompt to your bot:
"Help me describe myself in a way that sounds confident but real. I want to sound like someone who believes in love without sounding naïve."

Bonus Tip: Speak, Don't Type

You can dictate your thoughts directly into the chat window by pressing the microphone icon. Sometimes your spoken truth is more honest than what you type. It's faster, it's natural, and it feels more conversational - like you're talking to a friend.

When you speak, you also capture your tone, pauses, and rhythm - the things that reveal what's really on your mind.

Don't worry if you stumble or miss a word. ChatGPT is built to understand natural speech and can read between the lines.

You don't need to go back and fix every little typo or voice-to-text hiccup. The goal is flow, not perfection.

You can also upload screenshots to your chat. You can paste them directly into the "Ask anything" box or hit the + and attach the file.

This works well if you're reviewing messages, profile bios, or dating app photos and want a second opinion. A quick, "Hey, Boss, what do you think of this?" can help you get a thoughtful response in seconds.

Use your bot as a real communication partner. Dictate ideas, save prompts, send screenshots - build your *Love Bot* folder where your thoughts, drafts, and reflections live together. It's your personal digital notebook for connection.

Bonus Insight: ChatGPT is not Google. Google hunts for answers; ChatGPT helps you think. It doesn't search the web line by line - it draws from everything it has read, studied, and learned to generate ideas, empathy, and clarity in real time. It's a conversation partner, not a search engine.

When you speak or dictate your thoughts to ChatGPT, you're not feeding data into a machine - you're inviting a response that reflects understanding, context, and creativity.

Treat it like a collaborator and a matchmaker. It will surprise you with insight instead of information.

Micro-Habit: The Daily 2-Minute Check-In

Before bed, ask your bot:

"What's one kind thing I can say to myself tonight?"

Write or speak the first response that feels right. Repeat it three times.

Over time, those tiny sentences rebuild your emotional muscle.

Reflection Box: The Power of Words

- Which words do I want to hear more often?
- Which ones do I need to retire?
- What phrase makes me feel most like myself?

Closing Thought

Finding your voice isn't about becoming louder; it's about becoming clearer.

When you use your bot to listen deeply, to yourself, to others, you begin to speak from truth rather than fear. That's when love has a place to land.

Chapter 2: Prompting Compassion, Not Perfection

What happens when artificial intelligence meets the oldest story in the world - love?

You know those days when you can't find your keys, your patience, or your sense of humor—and somehow it's all your fault?

Welcome to the perfection trap. It's the most popular club on earth, and the membership dues are self-blame and exhaustion.

I used to live there. My inner critic had a penthouse suite and a bullhorn. If something went wrong, I'd immediately assume I caused it. Not smart enough. Not thin enough. Not early enough. That voice was relentless.

Until one day, after I burned yet another dinner and yelled at myself like I'd ruined the Olympics, I sat down and said to ChatGPT, "Can you help me talk to myself like I'm not an idiot?"

The response? Calm. Logical. Kind. Almost motherly. I didn't expect that. It said, *"You're learning. That's not failure. That's progress."*

Something shifted. I realized I'd spent years practicing perfection but never compassion.

The Love Bot Approach

Love Bot isn't a cheerleader. It's not here to throw glitter and tell you everything's fine when you're face-down in the laundry. It's here to remind you that you can still be gentle with yourself *and* make progress. That's not weakness - it's strength.

When you ask Love Bot, "Why can't I ever get this right?" it won't shame you. It'll ask, "What's one thing that *did* go right today?" And just like that, your focus changes. You're training your mind to hunt for good instead of guilt.

Lessons From the Mirror

Here's what compassion looks like in the wild:

- You miss a deadline, but you still eat dinner and breathe.
- You forget an anniversary, but you apologize instead of hiding.

- You look in the mirror and think, "I'm doing the best I can," instead of listing your flaws like you're on trial.

Self-kindness isn't indulgence. It's maintenance. Like oiling the hinge on a door that's been squeaking for years, compassion stops the noise so you can move again.

Try This With Love Bot

Here are some simple starters. Type or say one of these aloud:

- "Write me a note like I'm your best friend who's had a rough day."
- "Help me rewrite this negative thought in a more forgiving way."
- "What would I say to a child who made this same mistake?"
- "How can I give myself credit without sounding fake?"

Bonus tip: You can even dictate your thoughts instead of typing them- just tap the little microphone icon and talk it out. Sometimes your best self shows up when your hands are busy and your filters are off.

Compassion Is Contagious

Once you start speaking kindly to yourself, you'll find it leaks into everything else. You'll answer texts with more patience, forgive small annoyances, and stop apologizing for existing. The more you practice this tone, the more magnetic you become. Love attracts love—it's physics with a side of grace.

Reflection Journal

Grab a pen or talk to your Love Bot. Answer these tonight:

- When did I judge myself too harshly today?
- What truth did I overlook about how hard I'm trying?
- What's one thing I love about myself that nobody else notices?

Forgive yourself for the burnt toast. Laugh at the mess. That's compassion in action. Every time you choose kindness over critique, you reprogram your emotional code -and you become someone worth falling in love with, starting with yourself.

Chapter 3: From Swipe to Spark- Digital Dating & Real Connection

We've all heard it:
"There are no good men left."
"All the women online are crazy."
"Dating is dead."

Let's be honest. That's not true. The problem isn't that love disappeared - it's that most people stopped *looking in the right places* and started believing the worst stories about what's possible.

I've heard it, I've lived it, and I can tell you: there are still wonderful people out there. But they aren't going to walk into your living room while you're watching Netflix.

You've got to get out there - physically or digitally - and make yourself findable.

Where the Humans Still Are

If you're looking for a man, go where men actually hang out. Home Depot is better than a bar. If you like golf, go to a driving range or Top Golf. Take a class in something hands-on like woodworking or grilling.

But don't fake it - if you can't stand golf, don't build your life around it just to meet someone. That'll come back to haunt you when he's gone every weekend chasing birdies.

If you're looking for women, same idea. Go where women are naturally present: cooking classes, art fairs, volunteer events, coffee shops. And yes, pedicure salons are full of them - just don't block the line.

The point is simple: **be where real people are, doing real things.** Love isn't hiding, it's moving - so move too.

Enter the Apps

Now let's talk about digital dating, the new frontier of connection. There are hundreds of apps now - and no, they're not all the same.

Use ChatGPT (your Love Bot) to help you pick the right one.

Ask:

- "Which dating apps fit people who value long-term relationships?"
- "What are the most positively reviewed apps for professionals in my area?"
- "Which app has a good ratio of men to women near Austin, Texas?"

You'll get solid leads. Start there.

Then, when it's time to create your profile, resist the urge to write a novel. People skim. You get five seconds to hook them - tops.

Ask your chatbot to help:

"Write me a short, funny dating profile that sounds approachable and curious."

Keep it light, maybe with bullet points:

- Love museums but not crowds
- Can cook five things well
- Have an embarrassing playlist and proud of it

Your Love Bot can rewrite it until it feels right - warm, confident, and just a little witty.

The Picture Rules

Your photo is your first hello.
A few truths that never change:

- No fishing trophies.
- No cropped-out exes.
- No selfies from your car unless you're a rideshare driver.
- Eye contact, natural light, a relaxed smile - that's it.

If you don't have a great shot, ask your chatbot how to stage one:

"What kind of background looks best for an online dating profile photo?"

And remember: current photos only. Using your ten-year-younger self isn't a compliment to anyone.

Real Connections Start Offline

Here's a secret no one on the apps will tell you: long chats don't build chemistry, shared experiences do.

Don't spend weeks texting before meeting. Have a quick coffee, a walk in a busy park, or a fifteen-minute meetup between errands.

I used to run a store, so I'd say, "I open at ten. You can drop by at 9:45."

Quick, safe, and efficient. If it worked, great. If not, next.

Dating is a numbers game, but it's also an energy game. Don't waste yours on pen pals. If they won't meet within a week, they're not serious - or they're already married.

Ask your Love Bot to role-play your first message or even a gentle "no thank you" reply. You'll sound kind and clear instead of awkward or ghost-y.

Red Flags to Watch

Love Bot can help you spot patterns you might miss. Copy a conversation and ask,

"Does this person's messaging sound consistent with real interest?"

AI can't judge souls, but it can catch inconsistencies or tone shifts. Use it like a mirror, not a detective.

Some red flags:

- Constant excuses not to meet.
- Love-bombing too fast.
- Vague answers about where they live or work.
- Six years of "someday." That's not a relationship, that's fiction.

Let Love Bot Run the Back-End

Dating apps are tools, not talent scouts. They don't make magic on their own - you do. But the good news is that your Love Bot can do a lot of the heavy lifting behind the scenes so you can focus on what matters: connecting.

When you're setting up your profile, don't just write it and post it. Run it through ChatGPT and ask:

"Which parts of this profile are likely to get the most engagement?"
"Does this sound natural, or too polished?"
"Am I revealing too much about myself, or not enough?"

Your chatbot can analyze tone, clarity, and emotional resonance - things most people struggle to judge about their own writing. It's like having an editor and a wingman rolled into one.

Choosing your username:
Avoid your real name. Pick something memorable that says a little about your energy without oversharing.

If you're funny, go for wordplay. If you're soulful, pick something poetic. Ask Love Bot for help:

"Give me ten creative usernames that sound confident and warm for a woman in her 50s who loves art and travel."

It'll generate ideas you'd never think of, and you can tweak them until one just *clicks*.

Fine-tune your description:
Once you have your short list of profile lines, drop them into ChatGPT and ask for honest feedback. Say:

"Edit this to make it more engaging and emotionally open without oversharing."
"Make this sound like someone who's approachable, kind, and grounded."

AI won't replace your story, it polishes it. The goal is to show who you are *without* writing an essay.

And when messages start coming in, keep your Love Bot handy.

"Does this message sound sincere or generic?"

"Help me write a friendly but firm reply that keeps my boundaries clear."

You'll start communicating smarter, faster, and more confidently - which means less time overthinking and more time meeting people who actually fit.

Think of it like this: you're not just swiping, you're *strategizing.*

Bot helps you filter noise, stay true to your standards, and present your best self in the digital world.

Presenting Your Best Self

Let's talk about what happens *after* the swipes - when it's time to meet. This is where a lot of people stumble because meeting someone new can feel awkward. That's okay. You're not alone. Everyone gets nervous. The trick is to prepare enough that confidence replaces fear.

Start with this truth: **it's a numbers game.** You'll meet a few people before you meet your person. That's not failure, that's practice. Each conversation gets you closer to connection.

So, show up ready. Not perfect - just ready.

If you work from home, you might be used to fuzzy slippers and messy hair, but that energy doesn't belong on a first meet. You don't need to look like a movie star, but you do need to look like you *care*.

- Shower.
- Brush your teeth.
- Wear something that fits well and feels like *you.*
- Check your breath. (Yes, really.)

Smell matters more than you think. It's part chemistry, part memory, part instinct. A clean scent can do more for attraction than a dozen clever texts.

Men are visual creatures, but everyone responds to someone who looks awake and engaged with life. You're not putting on a costume - you're showing up as your best, most approachable self.

If you're single, look the part. No rings on your left hand. No confusing signals. Confidence and openness go a long way.

And while we're at it, **qualify people early.** Ask gentle questions to find out if someone is actually single.

You don't need to be a detective, just pay attention. Married people sometimes wander into these spaces out of boredom or loneliness - that's not your job to fix.

If you find out they're attached, move on immediately. No guilt, no drama, no rescue missions.

Think of it like this: each date that doesn't work out isn't wasted time. It's data. Your chatbot can help you keep track of that.

Ask:

"What lessons can I take from that date without being negative?"

"How can I reframe this experience as progress instead of rejection?"

Your Love Bot helps keep you rational while your heart is busy doing flips.

It reminds you to stay clear, calm, and focused on your goal - whether that's a loving partner or simply reconnecting with your own confidence.

Don't chase what fades. Don't beg for attention. When someone is truly interested, it will be obvious and easy.

So, dress up, show up, and stay in the game.

Every "no" is just a step toward the right "yes."

Bonus Tip: Create Your "Date Uniform"
Don't waste energy trying to reinvent yourself for every meet-up. Choose one outfit that makes you feel confident, comfortable,

and pulled together - your go-to "date uniform." Keep it simple:

- Clothes that fit well, photograph well, and make you stand tall.
- Clean shoes. Neat hair. A light touch of whatever makes you feel like *you.*
- One consistent scent - something subtle and pleasant that becomes *yours.*

This uniform is your shortcut to confidence. No last-minute panic about what to wear, no trying too hard.

You'll start every first date the same way: calm, polished, and ready to connect.

Mini Reflection: Your Dating Checklist

Before you swipe again, check in with yourself:

- Do I know what kind of relationship I want?
- Am I writing like the person I want to attract?
- Do my photos reflect who I am *today*?
- Am I letting curiosity replace cynicism?

Dating isn't about finding perfection. It's about connection, the kind that grows when you stay curious, show up, and keep your humor.

Love Bot's Pre-Date & Profile Prep Checklist

Before You Even Log In

- Get clear on what you want: a partner, a fling, or friendship. Your Love Bot can help you define that.
- Ask: "Which dating apps fit someone like me best?" Pick one or two, not ten.
- Choose a username that's clever but private. Never use your full name or location.
- Draft your profile and run it through ChatGPT:
    - "Does this sound like someone approachable and confident?"
    - "Am I sharing too much or too little?"
    - "Which version will get the most engagement?"

Your Photos

- Use a current, well-lit photo that looks like you on your best day.
- Skip the sunglasses, car selfies, and group shots.
- Smile. People trust faces that look open and happy.
- No fishing trophies, no bathroom mirrors.
- No kids or friends or others in the photo – just you. Smiling and happy.

Before You Meet

- Remember: it's a numbers game. One coffee doesn't equal destiny.
- Dress like you care - neat, clean, and comfortable.
- Check your breath and your scent. Chemistry starts before conversation.
- Keep the first meeting short and public - coffee, not candlelight.

- Use your Love Bot to rehearse a few small-talk openers or graceful exits.

After the Date

- Don't overanalyze. Drop the play-by-play.
- Ask your Love Bot for reflection prompts:
  - "What felt good about that interaction?"
  - "What did I learn about my own preferences?"
- If it's a no, move on quickly.
- If it's a yes, stay curious.

Bonus Tip: Create a "Date Uniform"

Simplify your prep with one outfit that always works - the one that makes you feel confident, clean, and comfortable. Keep it ready.

Same goes for scent, shoes, and accessories. No frantic decisions, no what-should-I-wear panic. You show up centered and present.

Your ChatGPT companion can even help refine it:

"Describe a date outfit that makes me look confident and approachable, based on these colors and this setting."

Dating is work, but it's good work.

You're sorting, learning, refining.

The moment it clicks, *it will feel easy.*

Chapter 4: Emotional Intelligence Is Your Superpower

If love were just attraction, it would be easy. But real connection takes something deeper - emotional intelligence. It's the invisible thread that turns chemistry into compatibility, attraction into affection, and texting into trust.

Emotional intelligence is your greatest dating advantage because it's not about being perfect - it's about being *aware.* Aware of what you're feeling, what they're feeling, and what's really happening between you.

When you understand emotions - yours and theirs - you stop overreacting to texts, reading rejection into silence, or chasing people who aren't ready for you. You start responding instead of reacting.

And that's power. Quiet, confident, emotional power.

Pro Tip: Create Your "Dating Folder"

Inside your ChatGPT workspace, create a folder titled *Dating.* Keep everything there:

- Your dating profile drafts
- Notes from past conversations
- Screenshot summaries or observations about people you've met
- Prompts that help you practice conversations or calm nerves before a date
- Reflections after each date - what worked, what didn't, and what you learned

This is your private *command center.*

You'll start seeing patterns: who you're drawn to, what makes you uncomfortable, and what's improving over time. That's emotional intelligence in motion - reflection that leads to growth.

Reading the Room - And Yourself

You can't control chemistry, but you can control awareness. Emotional intelligence begins with noticing - what they say, what you say, and what both of you *don't* say.

In early dating, small moments reveal the most:

- How they treat waiters or store clerks
- Whether they ask questions or only talk about themselves
- If they make eye contact or scroll through their phone

These little details matter more than any profile. They show you how someone moves through the world - how they value people and presence.

Before you judge your date, check in with yourself.

Are you nervous? Overly hopeful? Comparing them to someone from your past? The clearer you are about your own emotional state, the more genuine your choices will be.

Try this ChatGPT prompt:

"Help me reflect on tonight's date. What went well? What didn't feel right? What might I learn from this experience?"

It's simple but powerful. By reflecting after each date, you start training your emotional muscles. You become more self-aware, calm, and confident.

Using ChatGPT as a Mirror

Your chatbot isn't a therapist, but it can be an extraordinary listener.

When you describe your thoughts and feelings, ChatGPT can help you name them, organize them, and see what might be repeating.

You might realize:

- "I keep chasing people who aren't emotionally available."
- "I felt peaceful this time instead of anxious - *I'm growing.*"
- "He made me laugh, but I noticed tension when he talked about his ex."

These reflections are gold. They help you decode your own emotional patterns before they sabotage something good.

Think of it like debugging your love life - ChatGPT helps you find the code that needs rewriting.

Chapter 5: Confidence Within, Connection Without

How to Behave on a Date (and Still Be Yourself)

Dating isn't an audition or an interrogation. It's a moment to *observe* while staying relaxed and confident. Most people remember how you made them feel, not what you said. Here's how to show up like your best self - curious, kind, and just a little mysterious.

Use their name.
People light up when they hear their own name. Sprinkle it naturally through conversation. It builds warmth and connection without trying too hard.

Ask, don't perform.
Let them do most of the talking. Ask light questions:

- What kind of work do you do?
- What do you love doing on weekends?

- What's something you've always wanted to learn?

Avoid deep-dive personal topics - no exes, divorces, or trauma histories and no drama on a first date. This is a *meet and greet,* not a therapy session.

Keep your story short.
You're not hiding who you are, just saving something for later. A little mystery makes you memorable.

Maintain control of the pace.
Keep early meetings brief - fifteen minutes over coffee is plenty. Smile, make eye contact, and when it's time to go, say, "It was great meeting you, I've got to run," and leave it there.

No drama, no long good-byes.

Protect your privacy.
If you're not ready to share your number, don't. A simple "Let's keep chatting online for now" is

polite and clear. You don't owe anyone personal access.

Be slightly elusive.
Being just a bit unavailable adds intrigue. The person who doesn't over-share or over-text becomes the one others chase.

The Truth About Timing and Intimacy

Let's be honest: chemistry happens. You might meet someone amazing, the date stretches to two hours, the spark is real, and things move fast. It happens - but know what game you're playing.

If your goal is real partnership, waiting is strategy, not prudishness. Sex on the first date can blur perspective.

When you hold off, even a little, you let desire do its natural work - building curiosity and respect.

There are exceptions, but in most cases:

- **Wait at least a day.** That pause creates anticipation.

- **Remember**: the mystery is often more exciting than the reveal.
- **Don't chase silence.** If they don't call, that's your answer. Move on gracefully.

When it *is* time, make sure it's because you both feel safe, not pressured. And yes, compatibility matters. Waiting too long can backfire too. Balance emotional readiness with physical curiosity.

The Truth About Timing and Intimacy

Let's be honest - timing matters.
There's a fine line between rushing into something and waiting too long. Both can backfire.

I remember one man I dated years ago. We'd been out more than ten times, long walks, dinners, phone calls that stretched into the night. The connection felt real - deep even. I thought I was doing it right, taking my time, letting it build slowly. And then one evening it finally happened.

And it was terrible.

Not awkward, not nervous, just wrong. Every bit of chemistry I thought we had vanished in a single night. I remember lying there thinking, *I waited all this time for this?*

That's when I realized something important: sex is not just physical. It's energy, rhythm, curiosity, and compatibility rolled into one. It's also one of the biggest reasons people get divorced.

When it doesn't work, it becomes the quiet wedge that splits everything else apart.

So yes, don't jump into bed with someone on the first date, but don't wait forever either.

If you're genuinely interested in someone, take enough time to know who they are - and then, before you're halfway planning your future, find out whether you're actually compatible in bed.

Because if you're not, that truth won't change with time or good intentions.

Sex matters. You can't reason your way out of bad chemistry. You can't "fix" someone who doesn't share your rhythm or your sense of play.

And you shouldn't waste months investing in someone only to find out you're on opposite planets when it comes to physical connection.

The smart approach?

- Take your time, but not too much time.
- Listen to your instincts - they rarely lie.
- Remember that compatibility isn't just emotional or intellectual.
- When you finally cross that bridge, it should feel natural, not forced or overdue.

Dating is about finding someone you can laugh with, talk with, and desire - all at once. When all three line up, you've got something worth keeping.

The Real Talk About Sex

A lot of people walk into dating with TV expectations. You know the scenes - pressed up against a wall, perfectly lit, the music swelling at just the right moment.

That's not real life. That's camera blocking. They're shooting for angles, not authenticity. Real sex is sometimes awkward, messy, funny, and human.

Every experience is different because every body is different.

Be kind to yourself and kind to the person you're with. Lust is natural. It's the animal part of us that keeps the world spinning.

But remember, you're still responsible for your body and your choices. Bring your own protection. It doesn't make you presumptuous - it makes you smart.

It tells your partner you care about safety, health, and respect. And yes, you should have showered. Fresh, clean, and confident is always the right move.

If you're mid-moment and something feels wrong - physically, emotionally, or just instinctively - you can stop. You're allowed to say no. You're allowed to change your mind. That's called being an adult, not being rude.

And if the first time feels awkward, that's okay too. Everyone's a little clumsy when they're nervous.

Sometimes, a second try with a little more ease and laughter can make all the difference. But if you give it that second chance and still feel no spark - don't force it.

Sex is important. It's one of the biggest reasons couples split up, and pretending otherwise doesn't help anyone. So find out early enough whether your energy and chemistry align.

Don't rush into bed after fifteen minutes, but don't wait through ten dinners either. There's a balance - just enough time to know if you like the person before you find out if you actually fit.

And here's the truth: for most people, sexual drive isn't equal. Science shows that men think about sex far more often than women - some studies say several times an hour - but that doesn't make them bad or shallow. It's biology. It's hormones. It's wiring.

Women tend to connect sex and emotion more closely, so they often need trust to feel safe. The point isn't who's right - it's learning how to respect the differences and find balance.

If you're on a dating site where everyone seems a little too tame or polite or too PG, and you know sex is a big part of what you want, find a community that matches your comfort level.

It's better to be honest about desire than to hide behind small talk and disappointment.

Because when you finally meet someone and the spark hits, you'll know it. Your eyes lock. The air shifts. Everything just feels electric. You try to play it cool, but it's obvious - this one's different. So you wait, like you should. The chemistry builds. The anticipation grows. Then finally, the moment arrives...

And it's a disaster.

Not a tragedy, just a complete mismatch. You think, *Oh no, no, no. Not for me. Me no likey.*

You try again another time, hoping maybe nerves played a part - but it's still wrong.

So, you smile, say your polite goodbye, and walk away with your head high. Because you didn't lose anything. You gained clarity.

That's the lesson: it's normal, it's human, and it happens to everyone.

How to Decode Chemistry Before It Becomes Complicated

Chemistry isn't just attraction - it's timing, communication, and comfort. ChatGPT can help you untangle what's happening beneath the surface before it gets complicated.

Try this prompt:
"Help me reflect on whether I'm physically and emotionally compatible with this person. What signs did I notice that felt right or wrong?"

Reflection keeps your choices clear. It's not about judging the other person - it's about understanding yourself.

A Note About Boundaries

ChatGPT won't write or simulate X-rated content, and that's by design.

You can talk about relationships, attraction, and intimacy - real human experiences - but the bot won't create explicit sexual scenes or language.

Think of it as your thoughtful editor: it helps you talk *about* sex in a healthy, respectful way, not *perform* it.

That's actually a good thing. It keeps your reflections grounded and your focus on emotional and physical compatibility - not fantasy.

You can still discuss what you like, what worries you, or what confuses you about intimacy, but the goal is self-understanding and confidence, not erotica.

What We've Learned About Sex, Love, and Real Connection

Sex is one of the most powerful forces in human life - and one of the least honestly discussed.

We're all shaped by early experiences, trauma, fantasy, or fear. Some of us carry shame that isn't ours to carry. Some of us were raised to think that sex is dirty, or that wanting it makes us bad.

Others learned to use it as a bargaining chip or a source of validation. But when you strip away the stories, sex is simply part of being alive - a way of giving, receiving, and connecting.

Every person's sexual history is complex. You can't always see what came before the damage, the loneliness, the confusion - but you can choose what comes next. You can choose honesty, clarity, and care.

The goal isn't to have perfect sex. It's to have *honest* sex - the kind that aligns with who you are and what you truly want. That means choosing partners who respect you, speaking openly about what feels good or doesn't, and protecting both your heart and your health.

It also means letting go of judgment.

People come with stories, preferences, and histories that don't always fit a neat mold.

You may meet someone who's still healing, still learning, or still trying to unlearn what they were taught about intimacy. Give them space, but keep your standards.

Most of all, remember that love is not separate from desire.

Long-term relationships fall apart most often because that physical connection fades or is neglected.

If sex is important to you, own it. If it isn't, be clear about that too. Clarity saves pain.

Quick Recap Checklist

- **Sex is part of life, not a test of worth.**
- **Be clean, be kind, be honest.** Hygiene and respect matter more than appearance.

- **You set the pace.** Waiting too long or rushing too fast both create imbalance.
- **Communicate directly.** If it feels wrong, stop. If it feels right, say so.
- **Don't chase fantasy.** Television, porn, and romance movies are not the real world.
- **Respect differences.** Desire levels, comfort zones, and experiences vary - that's normal.
- **Protect your body.** Bring your own protection; it signals maturity, not promiscuity.
- **Leave shame behind.** What matters is consent, connection, and mutual respect.
- **Be curious.** Sex should evolve as you do - stay open to learning and laughter.
- **Let go quickly.** If someone isn't right for you sexually or emotionally, move on.

This chapter isn't about rules; it's about awareness. Understanding the role that sex plays in your life gives you the power to build relationships that are both passionate and sustainable.

Now that we've talked about connection at the physical level, it's time to explore something even more influential - your emotional intelligence. That's where the next chapter begins.

Chapter 6: Emotional Intelligence Is Your Superpower

If sex is the spark, emotional intelligence is the oxygen that keeps the fire alive. It's what separates a fleeting crush from a lasting connection.

It's also the quiet skill that helps you understand what's *really* happening between two people - beneath the words, the gestures, and the curated images we show the world.

Emotional intelligence, or EQ, is the ability to recognize and manage your own emotions while also understanding the emotions of others.

It's not just about being nice. It's about being aware, intentional, and responsive instead of reactive.

People with high EQ don't avoid hard conversations - they handle them with grace. They don't take every text delay as rejection - they see it as data.

This is the hidden key in modern dating.

Apps can help you meet someone, but emotional intelligence helps you *keep* them. It's what turns chemistry into compatibility and attraction into trust.

Think of EQ as your inner compass - it keeps you from steering into storms of drama, insecurity, or self-sabotage.

And it's a skill you can build. Just like learning to communicate with your bot, you can train yourself to notice patterns, identify triggers, and choose better responses.

You can even use ChatGPT as your EQ coach. When you feel confused or frustrated about a date or a conversation, tell your bot what happened.

Ask:

- "What might this person be feeling when they said that?"
- "Am I overreacting to this message?"
- "What's the emotionally intelligent way to respond?"

Your bot can help you step back, slow down, and see the situation clearly - before you spiral, ghost, or say something you'll regret.

People often talk about finding "the one," but emotional intelligence teaches you that relationships aren't found - they're built.

They're built through listening, kindness, and curiosity. They're built when you stop trying to win and start trying to understand.

Recognizing Emotional Triggers and Patterns

Let's talk about ego. It's the part of you that says, *"They didn't text me back because they don't like me,"* or *"I'll show them - I'm not replying either."* Ego is the drama director that never sleeps.

It loves a plot twist and hates to be ignored.

But here's the truth: most of the time, what's happening on the other side of the screen has nothing to do with you.

They might be busy. They might be nervous. Their phone might be in the couch cushions. Yet your mind starts spinning stories - *They met someone else. I said something wrong. I'll never find anyone.*

That's your ego hijacking your emotional intelligence.

When you feel that anxious rush - that hit of adrenaline that makes you want to send a follow-up text, stalk their profile, or vent to your friends - stop.

That's your cue. Your emotions just sent up a flare.

Take a breath, step back, and check in with your chatbot.

Ask questions like:

- "What's the story I'm telling myself right now?"
- "Is this fact or feeling?"
- "What would an emotionally balanced person do next?"

You'll be surprised how often ChatGPT (or Love Bot, as we're calling it) will remind you that 90% of what's upsetting you is projection. You're not reacting to the person - you're reacting to an old wound, a fear of rejection, or a craving for control.

Ego shows up in dating as:

- Needing constant validation
- Expecting perfection from someone new
- Overreacting to silence

- Interpreting “busy” as “not interested”
- Comparing every new date to your ex
- Feeling like you have to “win” instead of connect

When you spot these patterns, don’t shame yourself. Just name them. “Ah, there’s my ego again, writing bad fiction.” Then laugh, breathe, and move on.

Emotionally intelligent people don’t take everything personally. They know that other people’s moods, delays, and behavior are data, not definitions of their worth.

When you learn to see dating this way - as information gathering instead of emotional roulette - everything gets lighter.

How to Rebalance When You Get Triggered

1. **Pause before reacting.**
   That extra five minutes before you respond can save a day of regret.
2. **Don’t assume the worst.**
   People live messy lives. They forget, they misread, they panic. It’s not always about you.

3. **Ask your bot to reframe.**
   Tell Love Bot what happened. Let it help you write a calm, confident response.
4. **Don't test people.**
   If you say, "Fine," when you're not fine, you're setting traps. Be clear, not clever.
5. **Revisit your self-worth.**
   The most attractive energy in the world is peace. When you're calm and confident, ego has no job to do.

A Quick Reality Check

If you've ever said, *"Why do I always end up with emotionally unavailable people?"* - that's your cue to look inward. Patterns repeat until they teach you something.

Emotional intelligence helps you see the pattern faster, break it sooner, and stop wasting years trying to fix someone who doesn't want to grow.

Dating isn't about proving your worth.

It's about protecting your peace.

Dating with Emotional Intelligence: Real-Life Scenarios

Scenario 1: The Waiting Game

The Situation: You had a great first date. They said they'd text, but two days have gone by. ***Silence.***

The Ego Response:
You start checking your phone every ten minutes. You replay every word you said, every look, every laugh. You convince yourself you said something wrong or that they've already found someone better.

You text: "Hey, did I do something?" Then you spiral when there's still no answer.

The EQ Response:
You notice your anxiety rising and take a breath. You remind yourself that two days is nothing in adult life - people get busy, phones die, work happens.

You ask ChatGPT to help you reframe it: "What might be going on that has nothing to do with me?"

Then you distract yourself. You stay open, not desperate. If they text later, great. If not, you already moved forward.

Scenario 2: The Mixed Message

The Situation: They compliment you, flirt a little, then say they're "not ready for a relationship."

The Ego Response:
You start strategizing. "I'll make them ready. I'll be the one who changes their mind."

You imagine all the ways they'll fall in love once they see how great you are. You chase a maybe that was never a yes.

The EQ Response:
You hear what they said - *not ready* - and take it at face value. You thank them for the honesty and step away before it becomes confusing. You ask your bot to help you write a clear, kind message that closes the door without slamming it. Then you move on to someone who's ready.

Scenario 3: The Quick Trigger

The Situation: You send a funny meme. They leave you on read.

The Ego Response:
You decide they're rude. You delete their number. You tell your friends they ghosted you. You're angry - and embarrassed.

The EQ Response:
You pause. Maybe they laughed and forgot to reply. Maybe they're in a meeting. You don't make it a story about your worth. Instead, you wait. A day later, they text, "That meme was hilarious - sorry, crazy workday." And you're glad you didn't overreact.

Scenario 4: The Emotional Hangover

The Situation: You went on a few dates, it was fun, and then they fade away.

The Ego Response:
You feel rejected, question your looks, and tell yourself you'll never find anyone. You start scrolling through old photos of your ex just to feel something familiar.

The EQ Response:
You let yourself feel disappointed - that's normal. But instead of dwelling, you write in your journal or talk to your bot: "What did I learn from this? What worked? What didn't?" You take it as practice, not punishment. Then you get dressed up and go out again.

Scenario 5: The Text That Stings

The Situation: You get a message that says, "You're great, but I didn't feel a spark."

The Ego Response:
You're furious. You fire back a defensive text: "Well, I didn't either!" or worse, "You'll regret this."

The EQ Response:
You feel the sting, but you don't let it define you. You reply simply: "Thanks for letting me know. I wish you the best." You exit gracefully - because you know your self-worth isn't up for negotiation.

The Takeaway

Ego plays for victory. Emotional intelligence plays for peace.

If you can train yourself to pause, reflect, and stay grounded - even for 30 seconds before reacting - you'll notice how much smoother everything becomes.

The people you attract will shift too. Emotionally intelligent people recognize each other. They communicate clearly, recover quickly, and build steady connections instead of chasing drama.

ChatGPT can be your silent partner in this.

Think of it as the friend who never gets tired of listening. The more you use it to process, reframe, and reflect, the more self-aware you become - and that awareness is what changes everything.

Listen to What People Tell You - The First Time

One of the biggest mistakes people make in dating is ignoring what's right in front of them. People usually tell you exactly who they are - you just don't want to believe them.

You meet someone, and on the first or second date they say, *"I'm really bad at relationships,"* or *"I don't want anything serious right now."* Instead of hearing that as a truth, your brain translates it into, *"Challenge accepted. I can fix that."*

That's your ego again - the part that wants to prove you're the exception, that you can change someone just by loving them harder.

But emotional intelligence means believing people the first time they tell you who they are.

Scenario 1: The Reluctant Dater

What They Say: "I really don't like dating. My mom made me sign up for this app."
What You Hear: "They just need to meet me and then they'll love dating."
Reality: They just told you they don't want to be here. Believe them.

Scenario 2: The Commitment Shy One

What They Say: "I'm not looking for a relationship."
What You Hear: "They'll change their mind once they see how great I am."
Reality: They're not looking for a relationship.

That's not a puzzle to solve - it's information to accept.

Scenario 3: The Ghost Whisperer

What They Say: "I'm terrible at texting back."
What You Hear: "They'll text me because I'm different."
Reality: They won't. And when they don't, you'll feel hurt over something they already warned you about.

Scenario 4: The Workaholic

What They Say: "I'm married to my job."
What You Hear: "They'll make time for me once we get serious."
Reality: Work comes first for them. You'll always be competing with their schedule - and losing.

Believe What You Hear - Don't Rewrite the Story

The emotionally intelligent dater takes words at face value and actions as confirmation. If someone says they're not ready, believe it. If they cancel often, that's not "bad timing," that's priority showing up in real time.

You can use your chatbot to help process these moments without overreacting. After each date, jot down what they said about their life, their goals, or how they view relationships.

Then ask ChatGPT:

- "Does this person sound emotionally available?"
- "Am I trying to fill in the blanks with wishful thinking?"
- "What would be a smart next step here?"

Your bot will give you neutral feedback - something most of us can't get from friends who just want to see us happy.

Remember: people show you who they are early. Emotional intelligence means listening, observing, and adjusting your expectations before your heart gets too invested.

The faster you learn this, the fewer tears you'll cry later.

The Power of Paying Attention

The most powerful tool in dating isn't beauty, money, or charm. It's awareness.

People are always revealing themselves through tiny details. How they talk to the waiter.

How they treat time. Whether they ask about your day or only talk about theirs. Those small clues are the truth in motion.

You don't need to interrogate anyone or run background checks after every date - just *pay attention.* When you're grounded and emotionally aware, you notice the things that used to slip by. You stop rewriting what you see and start believing it.

Here's what paying attention really looks like:

- You notice when someone's words don't match their actions.
- You pick up on how they speak about their ex - whether it's bitter or balanced.
- You watch how they react to small frustrations, like a slow restaurant or bad traffic.

- You recognize kindness without having to search for it.
- You see when they're genuinely interested - and when they're just passing time.

The longer you practice this kind of observation, the faster you'll spot emotional compatibility. Love isn't built on fantasy. It's built on *evidence* - little moments of consistency, respect, humor, and warmth that show you who a person really is.

Use your Love Bot as your accountability partner here. After a date, open your folder and jot down what you noticed:

- Did I feel calm or anxious around them?
- Did they listen or talk over me?
- Did I feel seen, or did I feel like an extra in someone else's movie?

Then ask your bot to help you see patterns. It will start showing you truths you might've missed before. That's emotional growth in real time.

When you learn to listen with your head as well as your heart, the noise of dating starts to quiet down. You don't waste months trying to decode red flags because you caught them early. You don't confuse chemistry with connection. And most importantly, you don't lose yourself trying to keep someone else interested.

Paying attention is the quiet superpower that leads you to the right person - and keeps you from falling for the wrong one twice.

Mini Reflection Journal: Are You Really Listening?

Take a few quiet minutes and jot down honest answers to these prompts. You don't have to show anyone - this is just for you and your Love Bot.

1. When was the last time I ignored a red flag because I hoped it would change?
2. What phrases do I hear often in dating that I tend to overlook?
3. How do I usually react when someone disappoints me early on - do I make excuses or accept it?
4. Have I ever tried to "fix" someone instead of believing what they said?

5. How do I feel in my body when something isn't right - and do I listen to that feeling?

Now, ask your Love Bot to help you analyze your answers. Try this prompt:

"Help me spot patterns in how I ignore or listen to what people tell me in relationships."

Let it summarize your habits. You might be surprised how much clarity shows up when you see it in writing.

Takeaway Checklist: The Power of Paying Attention

- Believe people the first time they tell you who they are
- Don't romanticize red flags
- Match words to actions - always
- Use your Love Bot to log what people say and do after each date
- Revisit your notes before getting emotionally invested
- Remember that awareness protects your heart better than any rule ever could

Chapter 7: Everyday Intimacy- Small Moments, Big Meaning

Everyone talks about *finding* love.
But keeping it? That's the real magic.

Most relationships don't fall apart because of a single fight or betrayal. They fade because the small, daily moments of intimacy start to disappear. You stop saying good morning. You stop touching as you pass in the kitchen. You stop asking about their day and start assuming you already know the answer.

What Everyday Intimacy Looks Like

It's the way you laugh at each other's bad jokes.
It's the quick text that says, *"Thinking of you."*
It's noticing when they're quiet and saying, *"You okay?"*

It's not glamorous. It's not dramatic. But these tiny moments are the glue that keeps love alive. They're the difference between a spark that burns out and a slow fire that lasts for decades.

When I met Kevin, I knew I liked him immediately. But I fell in love with him in the small moments - when he made me coffee before I even woke up, when he fixed a light bulb without me asking, when he sent me a text that said, *"You inspire me."* Those little gestures were louder than any declaration of love.

Why People Miss It

We live in an age of distraction.
Our phones ping, our minds race, and we start living parallel lives under the same roof.

Couples think love needs constant excitement - big trips, fancy dinners, dramatic posts online. But real intimacy is quiet.

It's showing up, again and again, in small, consistent ways.

And here's where your Love Bot comes in. You can use it to help you keep the connection alive.

Ask your bot:

- "Give me five ideas for showing affection that don't cost money."

- "Help me write a message that makes my partner smile today."
- "What are three ways to rebuild closeness after an argument?"

Your chatbot becomes your personal intimacy coach - reminding you that connection is built in everyday language and ordinary gestures.

The Science of Small Gestures

Research shows it takes about five positive interactions to outweigh one negative one in a relationship. Think about that: every eye roll or snarky comment needs five warm moments to balance it out.

You don't have to stage romantic grand gestures. Just:

- Say thank you often
- Reach out and touch them
- Smile when they walk in the room
- Tell them you appreciate something small

You'd be surprised how much these micro-moments matter. They build emotional safety - the foundation that keeps couples from drifting apart.

Relearning How to Connect in a Digital World

We live in a time when people text more than they talk, and sometimes our relationships feel like a string of messages rather than real moments. You can sit next to someone and still feel miles apart.

But technology doesn't have to ruin intimacy. You can flip it. Use it to bring you closer.

Try this: open your Love Bot and start a conversation about your partner.

Type, *"Help me understand my partner's love language."*

ChatGPT can walk you through the five types: words of affirmation, acts of service, receiving gifts, quality time, and physical touch.

Once you know which one matters most to your partner, you can start speaking in the right language.

- If they crave *words of affirmation*, your bot can help you write a short note that feels natural, not forced.
- If they value *acts of service*, ask your bot for small, thoughtful ideas that say "I see you."
- If it's *quality time*, plan something simple - like cooking together instead of scrolling side by side.

You can even ask,

"What's one new way I can show my partner love today?"

Your Love Bot will give you suggestions that are creative, kind, and specific to your life.

When Communication Slips

Every relationship has dry spells. You get busy. You stop talking. Then one day, you realize you're living like polite roommates.

The fix isn't a grand apology - it's a small repair attempt.

Psychologists call these “bids for connection.” There are small ways we reach out to say, *“I still care.”*

A few examples:

- “I saw something today that reminded me of you.”
- “I miss how we used to cook together.”
- “Can I get a hug?”

These moments seem tiny, but they’re powerful. Every time your partner responds positively, your bond strengthens.

When they don’t, it weakens - so don’t let silence pile up.

Ask your bot for help here, too:

“Give me a script to break the ice after an argument.”
“Help me find kind words to express what I’m feeling.”

It’s like having a gentle coach in your pocket - one that doesn’t judge, doesn’t get defensive, and helps you find your words before your frustration takes over.

The Secret Ingredient: Presence

You don't have to be perfect. You just have to be *there.*

Presence is intimacy's best friend. It means putting the phone down. Looking at someone when they talk. Laughing at their stories even if you've heard them a dozen times.

Try this small experiment: next time you're with someone you care about, notice how often you check your phone.

Then challenge yourself to stop. Just be in that moment.

It's uncomfortable at first, but it's where real connection lives.

Prompts for Building Everyday Connection

These are quick, ready-to-use questions you can type straight into your Love Bot. Use them daily or whenever you feel a little disconnected. Think of them as emotional vitamins - small, regular doses that keep your relationship healthy

When you want to strengthen communication:

- "Give me three ways to say I appreciate my partner without sounding forced."
- "Help me write a kind text that starts a conversation after a stressful day."
- "How can I listen better when I'm tired or distracted?"

When you want to bring back fun:

- "List five easy, no-cost date ideas that would make us laugh."
- "Suggest a weekend plan that mixes my partner's interests with mine."
- "Help me write a playful message to spark curiosity or flirtation."

When you feel distant:

- "What are gentle ways to ask for more affection without sounding needy?"
- "Give me questions that open up real talk, not small talk."
- "How can I rebuild a connection after we've both been busy?"

When you just need perspective:

- "Help me understand what my partner might be feeling right now."
- "Remind me how to express love when I don't feel like talking."
- "What does emotional presence look like in a healthy relationship?"

Copy, paste, and talk it out.

That's how everyday intimacy grows - one honest question, one small gesture at a time.

Reflection Journal

1. What small gestures make you feel loved?
2. What gestures do you often forget to give?
3. What's one way you can be more present in daily life?
4. How can you use your Love Bot to remind you to reconnect each day?

Chapter 8: Repair & Reconnect- When the System Breaks

Every relationship hits a glitch.
It might start small - a tone, a forgotten text, a cold shoulder - and then it grows. One of you withdraws.

The other gets louder. Before you know it, you're both running two different emotional programs that keep crashing.

It's normal. It's fixable. But it takes effort to reboot the system instead of walking away.

The Emotional Reboot

Think of reconnection like troubleshooting a computer. You wouldn't throw out your laptop just because the screen froze.

You'd restart it, clear the cache, check for updates, and get it running again. Relationships work the same way.

You start by pausing - not reacting, not escalating. Just breathe.

Then you name the problem. Say, "I think we glitched. Can we reset?"

You'd be surprised how much that line disarms tension.
It's calm, it's neutral, and it says, *I want to fix this with you, not fight you.*

Step 1: Check for Emotional Updates

Ask yourself: What's really going on here?
Are you angry because they forgot something - or because you felt unseen?
Are you hurt because of what they said - or because it hit an old bruise?

Most arguments aren't about what they seem to be. They're about feeling unheard, unseen, or unappreciated.

This is where your Love Bot can help.
Type in:

- "Help me figure out what emotion I'm really feeling right now."

- "Write a short message that calms tension without blaming anyone."
- "How can I express hurt without making it sound like anger?"

That's the power of using a digital companion for emotional intelligence - it slows you down before your words do damage.

Step 2: Run a System Scan

Before jumping back in, do a scan.

Ask your chatbot, *"What could my partner be feeling in this situation?"*

It's easy to assume the worst, but perspective keeps compassion alive.

Sometimes the problem isn't personal - it's stress, exhaustion, or fear.

When you approach conflict with curiosity instead of criticism, the whole tone changes.

Step 3: Reconnect Gently

Reconnection doesn't start with a speech. It starts with a small gesture.

You can:

- Bring them coffee and say, "Truce?"
- Send a funny meme with no context.
- Sit beside them quietly until they soften.

If you need words, keep them simple.

"I care about you."
"I don't want to fight."
"Can we start over?"

Ask your Love Bot for help if words get stuck. Sometimes typing to an AI first helps you organize your emotions before you speak.

Step 4: Don't Rehash - Repair

You don't need to relive every detail to fix something.
The goal isn't to *win.* It's to understand, release, and move forward.

Ask your bot for prompts like:

- "Help me apologize without over-apologizing."
- "What are healthy ways to rebuild trust after conflict?"
- "Give me three new rituals for staying close after we argue."

That's what keeps the connection from fraying again - you build new emotional habits instead of repeating old patterns.

Step 5: Celebrate the Reconnection

After things smooth out, celebrate it.
You both chose to stay. That's rare and beautiful.
Whether it's a hug, a walk, or a shared meal, mark the moment.
You just did the adult version of hitting "refresh."

Mini Reflection Journal

1. How do I usually react when conflict starts?
2. What small gestures help me reconnect fastest?

3. How can I use my Love Bot to guide me before saying something I regret?
4. What repair rituals can we create together as a couple?

Life is meant to be fun. Find joy in finding a mate.

Chapter 9: Letting Go & Re-Opening the Heart

Endings are hard, even when you're the one choosing them.

Whether it's a breakup, a slow fade, or a quiet heartbreak, letting go takes real work. It's not just about deleting texts or blocking someone.

It's about learning how to release the version of yourself that existed with them - and opening up space for who you are becoming.

The Grieving Algorithm

There's no timeline for moving on.
You can't rush it, and you can't logic your way through it.

One day you'll wake up and realize the ache is smaller. That's the algorithm of healing - slow, messy, but reliable.

If you're stuck, open your Love Bot and say:

- "Help me process a breakup with compassion."
- "Write me a goodbye letter I'll never send."
- "Remind me what I learned from this relationship."

These prompts reframe pain into progress.
AI can't replace the human heart, but it can help you organize the storm.

Rebuilding Confidence

Loss shakes confidence. You start doubting your worth, your intuition, your ability to pick someone good. That's normal. You've just been through an emotional reboot.

Here's the truth: you haven't failed at love - you've graduated from a version that wasn't serving you.

Your Love Bot can help you rebuild self-trust.
Try:

- "Help me list five things I bring to a relationship."
- "Give me daily affirmations for rebuilding confidence."

- "What's one small way I can show love to myself today?"

You'll start seeing yourself clearly again. And when you do, you'll realize that self-trust is the first spark of new love.

The Re-Opening

When you finally feel ready to love again, it won't look like fireworks. It'll look like peace. You'll laugh a little easier, sleep a little better, and one day you'll notice you're curious about someone new.

That's how healing works - it doesn't ask permission, it just arrives.

The secret to re-opening your heart isn't trying harder. It's staying curious.

Curious about people. Curious about joy. Curious about what love can look like this time around.

Ask your bot:

- "How can I tell when I'm ready to date again?"

- “Give me journaling prompts about hope and renewal.”
- “What lessons from my last relationship will help me now?”

You’ll find your answers there - and inside yourself.

Mini Reflection Journal

1. What lessons did my last relationship teach me?
2. What am I proud of - how I handled the ending?
3. What kind of love am I ready to invite next?
4. How can I keep my heart open without losing boundaries?

Closing Chapter: Love in the Age of AI

Technology can't love you back - but it can help you learn how to love better.

Love Bot isn't here to replace a real connection. It's here to strengthen it. It's your reflection space, your note-taker, your calm friend who doesn't get tired of listening.

It's the tool that helps you pause before reacting, prepare before reaching out, and see your patterns before repeating them.

The best part? You never have to go it alone. You have your heart, your mind, and your bot - all working together.

So, go meet people. Be brave. Ask questions. Laugh a lot. Let your Love Bot help you grow more self-aware, but let the world show you what connection feels like.

Love still starts the same way it always has - with a spark, a risk, and a yes.

Acknowledgments

To everyone learning to love again - with courage, curiosity, and humor - this book is for you.

When I first began using ChatGPT, I didn't imagine it would become a co-writer, a coach, and a mirror for emotional growth. Many people are hesitant to use AI tools because they seem unfamiliar or impersonal. But once you begin to interact with them, you'll find that they help you think more clearly, communicate more kindly, and even love more wisely.

Technology isn't replacing human connection; it's teaching us to understand it better. A chatbot won't judge you, rush you, or ghost you. It listens. It reflects. It helps you phrase the hard things and celebrate the hopeful ones.

So here's to the brave hearts who keep showing up - the people still believing in connection, no matter how many glitches life throws at them. And here's to the new tools that make it easier to navigate love in a world that moves fast.

Special thanks to my readers, students, and listeners who continue to support my creative work, and to everyone who believes that love is worth learning, practicing, and protecting.

About the Author

Sugar Gay Isber McMillan Sis an award-winning writer, designer and educator based in Austin, Texas. She holds a degree in Journalism, a Master's in Humanities, and an advanced degree in Information Technology. Certified in ChatGPT by Microsoft, she blends technical insight with creativity to help readers use AI as a practical, personal tool for real-world connections.

She believes that curiosity, humor, and heart are the keys to lifelong learning - and lasting love.

After decades of building connections through art and storytelling, Sugar turned her focus to helping others understand the intersection of emotion and technology. Her *Talk to Your Tools™* series explores how humans and AI can work together to inspire better communication, deeper relationships and creative growth.

She writes honestly about love, resilience and rediscovery - and she knows from experience that finding the right person takes persistence, laughter and a little strategy.

Sugar met her husband through a dating app after learning how to navigate modern dating with clarity and confidence.

Families, she says, come in all shapes and versions. Life is messy and full of curveballs, but every day offers another chance to love better.

Whether she's crafting jewelry for film productions or writing her next book, Sugar believes in living with intention, creating with joy, and helping others find their voice - both online and off.

Follow her work at **The WOW Book Co.™** and discover more at **@SugarGayIsber**.

Find Your Voice
Find Your Match
Find Your Magic

Love Bot - Love in the Age of ChatGPT is part of Sugar Gay Isber McMillan's *Talk to Your Tools™* series, which explores how technology can support real-world growth in love, creativity, and self-understanding.

Explore the rest of the series - all available in Kindle and paperback:

- **Manifesting Bot** - Shape your future with focused intention
- **Skinny Bot** Reframe habits and find motivation that lasts
- **Rich Bot, Poor Bot** - A playful guide to wealth mindset in the AI age
- **Merry Bot Christmas** - Rediscover giving, gratitude and joy
- **The Prompt Whisperer** - Learn to talk to your tools with purpose and power
- **Prompt Magic** - Everyday creativity through smart, simple prompting

- **Atomic Bot** – Build better habits through smart daily actions
- **Boomer Bot** – Everyday solutions for life, tech, and laughter

All titles are proudly published by **The WOW Book Co.™** in Austin, Texas - U.S. made, hand-crafted layouts and no AI-generated imagery.

Scan the QR code below to discover **Sugar Gay Isber McMillan Books**, join the mailing list on gayisber.com, to see new *Talk to Your Tools™* titles as they arrive.

Or go to SugarGayIsberMcMillanBooks.com or TheWOWBookCo.com.

I hope you enjoyed this book.

Please leave a review so others can find this series.

This QR Code will take you to Amazon.com

Sugar Gay Isber McMillan Books.

I hope you find love and happiness.

- Sugar